20 QUESTIONS

Other Books by Dennis Phillips:

Arena
Means
A World
The Hero Is Nothing

DENNIS PHILLIPS | 20 QUESTIONS

For Richard,
for (his) with
troubles,
all best,
Dennis
St. P's day 1993

Jahbone Press
Los Angeles

Copyright © 1992 Dennis Phillips
All rights reserved

Book design by Robin Palanker

Library of Congress Cataloguing in Publication Data

Phillips, Dennis
    Twenty Questions

1. Title

ISBN: 0-9629903-0-2

5 4 3 2 1

Some of these questions appeared in *Re-map*. Thanks to the editors.

The author thanks the MacDowell Colony and the Rockefeller Foundation's Bellagio Study Center for residencies during which *Twenty Questions* was written.

Jahbone Press
3787 Maplewood Avenue
Los Angeles, California 90066

20 QUESTIONS

ONE

Given their approximate ages.

The way to the dancers is across an impossible lawn.

They invented a formula which compared depth to credit.

Across the foundation were strewn the ruins of an ancient village.

To be truly wide-ranging.

The meaning of a sentence has been the object of a divisive argument.

These lines will be determined by the specific needs of a computer's program for page design.

A monument had been erected to memorialize a murdered hero.

Probably they had remembered to bring vitamins.

After a certain age routine threatens to replace philosophy, ethics and even pleasure.

Viewed from the proper angle anyone's anthropomorphic version of the giant rock could at least be understood.

And so they burned the village to the ground; a strong message you might say.

Others say that thorn bushes were imported as a means of forcing the natives to wear shoes.

A certain species of fish called parrot fish constantly excrete white sand which they produce by eating coral.

Perseverance will not always help.

Reading as opposed to interpreting the signs.

Elevation and the payment of debts could also be fit into the theory.

Some thought that the hero's arriving at the time of the predicted arrival of a god was mere co-incidence.

It is suggested that one island's beaches once passed through the bowels of a fish.

Only because of an unjustifiable instinct.

TWO

Nothing in his life became him like the leaving it.

If the subject is weather.

Casting spells will work more efficiently under water.

The flowers they sent were cloying— the smell, not the appearance.

There will likely always be a sacrificial character.

The boredom of the capitalist or the self-assuredness of the capitalist.

You may stir the beakers and hope for a settling effect later.

Looking into the crevices and cracks they missed the larger creatures which traveled silently past them.

Because density.

If they fall asleep during dinner ask the Maitre d' to escort them to the door.

It is hoped that the winds will stop.

The launch was sent to the ship but the passengers could not make their way on board.

Although the leader was very self-conscious, there was no reason to risk anyone's safety.

Looking out for the larger creatures they missed the tiny creatures which live in the crevices and cracks.

As complicated as the knots it untangles.

Any action, any thought, any feeling, any analysis, any memory, any word, any opening.

On the south side a truce was finally reached.

They preferred windows to be left opened once they determined that the sound they heard was the ocean's and not the giant fans of the air conditioning.

Fluency in the rituals was not enough to admit them.

Tell them not to yell, a system is moving in, sacrifices must be made ahead of the first squall.

THREE

They will not violate the wind line.

The view is so wide not only the whispers were accompanied by strings.

Were a small voice to tell you to stop.

Where depth and height seem similar.

Is this the end of your vacation she asked or was asked.

To believe in something even infinities.

Realizing that their meals would come separately, they requested that the captain circle the harbor until they both had finished eating.

Some of them actually endorsed an astro-meteorological view of creation.

She said my boyfriend has checked in or out already she was told.

In an age where transportation.

The gale had ripped ancient trees from the ground and wouldn't permit their hair to stay in place.

In the satisfied and accepting gaze of parenthood.

The person is generic.

They had sealed what they thought were the seams and the wind was not deterred.

From the peak of the bay the clarity was so great that even the driest comment vibrated like the reeds of an oboe.

The work is a compilation of one person's way of writing influenced by events, sensations, other writers, who, in turn, were so influenced.

You can speak and yet the magnitude of geography.

Gliding at a 90 degree angle caused their blood to settle in odd places.

Even the constant effect of the parrot fish in building.

Windows then, a couple of flat notes, three callings before a punchline, the rejection of punchlines.

FOUR

Though the hieroglyphics were cogent, the message was disheartening; so much so that the decoders promised to confess ignorance and were seen as failures, but not for the right reasons.

In the mode of hysteria we would include both laughter and sexual hyperactivity, uncontrolled anxiety and the constant desire to eat.

Thus they gathered together each year in groups of 10 to 40 and professed truths to each other which were or were not enduring.

Being lowered into the crypt was not frightening until their feet touched the ground.

The equivalent was found in leaders of powerful countries who chose to invade other countries to solve temporary problems known only through surveys.

The woman at the party was concerned about the idea of lyricism.

The precision of their maps was of little use.

You may choose to sing but how the words are taken is never certain.

Some idea must lie behind such aberrant behavior, they thought.

Though the hieroglyphics were cogent the message was disheartening; so much so that although the decoders promised to return to work the next day, they were never heard from again.

It is a time of the year, it is always a time of the year.

It was so dark their lights were drunk up by the depth; no one could help them if the safety devices failed.

Perhaps the remnant of an ancient war.

Legalities were never an issue before the myth of democracy forced the invention of more elaborate lies.

They refused to operate, but then removed whatever they could.

Take / report / undertake / invade

Everyone they had known from a certain period of their pasts had been invited and most showed up.

Once at the bottom of the crypt it took them thirty three days to discover where the "Written Wall" was.

Across the hall from the concert a small exhibition had been installed that cast an angle of interpretation on the music that could never have been imagined.

There was rarely a problem striking up an amusing conversation.

FIVE

There is a temper of atmosphere which prevents rain.

The fear of random gunshots kept them indoors.

His only consolation was that he knew she would think of him sometime during the day.

To arrive on time is only a shame in certain countries.

They could agree on movies but realized this was nothing.

Preferably during sex.

The substance so wished for which falls, runs, or exudes.

There were the few concerns they took with them into the new decade although some argued that the decade wouldn't begin for a year.

Such celebrations were common only in the most violent societies such as the United States and El Salvador and Lebanon.

The inexorable passage of time.

The recent orgy of biographical readings served to set his mind at ease — some of the other geniuses.

It would be simpler just to say that nothing had happened.

In projecting the response to new forms the oddest alliances were considered.

Or after sex then.

A drought could last a whole decade taking deceptive forms such as deluge or ozone depletion.

Back east it snowed severely.

Some event which he knew to have been traumatic was beyond his ability to remember.

The ritual then, in and of itself.

Held as sacred the first phial of liquid was sand in her dream of drawers.

Just think of the potential.

SIX

There is never the proper record.

Although warned repeatedly, no one was prepared for the lack of "sanitation facilities."

Open-ended debate was what the local politicians feared more than anything.

Some people forget to place a small fish in the ground before they plant.

She had said, but really more to herself than anyone else, "Damn! What else could I forget?!"

The constant rolling of the swells began to effect even the most experienced of the sailors, except the skipper, who ate pork and beans with impunity.

Positioning, in general, is the overriding concern.

Open-ended debate was what the national politicians feared more than anything.

Saving canceled checks for at least eight years.

You may doubt the importance of political action groups, but money speaks, we are told.

Or the shear act of remembering how many times any single idea had occurred.

The picture is complete in the reader's mind with very little help from the writer.

As the aboriginal tribes of the American North East knew.

The famous author had the foresight to save the lists used in writing so that scholars could later make much of these records, and so that they could be sold, these lists that is.

Be careful never to underline passages in books which may later be used as evidence against you.

Literally no one had remembered to bring a camera.

In their calculations only interruptions had been overlooked.

No matter where the boat is some contact must be made.

Even people with photographic memories.

How much Schliemann wrecked on his way through Hissarlik to find Troy.

SEVEN

The attachment of the heart to the diaphragm.

References from unsubstantiated events were omitted.

At the ceremonies the feather-robed one was always in charge.

From the top, a vast blanket of rain forest.

Then indentation determines everything.

Arriving on time was not even a question.

Though several areas were left open for speculation.

These symptoms were only the result of urbanity.

Pulling the active heart from the dazed citizen was always the most exciting part.

Who could believe the wisdom of anyone wearing such an expensive suit.

Continuously making decisions which go against its best interests.

Slaves had built the edifice with stone quarried from sites selected by priests.

One's very survival.

When the view withheld details the residue was dark houses where everyone slept.

In case anyone cares, the books will be left on reserve.

They believed that the sudden death of a friend had no relation to themselves.

Once opened, the chest was a disorganized mess of blood and moving tissue, except to those who knew.

Though the fastest way down was lethal.

Records will be relegated to a single meaning.

Or the total anatomy, displayed in parts with overlays of acetate.

EIGHT

Deductions will not be permitted.

Although they ask questions, a quantity of fluid exudes from their friendliness.

The choice of foods.

We asked politely and reasoned smoothly.

Wives must not have been considered by some.

There will always be a surprise, not usually welcomed.

One had long legs and tight pants.

They had required variegated behavior from each person.

Notice was always given in advance through the mail.

What they had meant by deductions was a form of logic, but many understood it to refer to income tax.

Great concern was manifest regarding the ownership of baggage.

Control, lack of control, surrender of control.

The wax they mold to their faces despite the anniversary.

Seeking answers would negate specific powers.

A year later, what was thought a trivial comment was remembered with resentment and anger by a long-forgotten acquaintance.

It was only a job and yet the very specter of the company was at least intimidating and perhaps inspiring.

The idea of velocity, the sensation of speed, the realization of altitude, the image of destination.

No order was specifically indicated.

It was easier to simply remain quiet.

Of course it could never be possible to remember all the people one has met.

NINE

A clock must be brought.

Noticing the exact anniversary.

Then space.

The approach of warmer weather heralded by slower cars.

The policeman assigned to the case preferred to chat with the editor of a local Cuban magazine.

No single set of criteria.

Falling asleep would be easy and calm although lore of the region placed the sleeper at some jeopardy.

Perhaps there is always one who must appear dominant because of fear.

Facing west all day gives an unreliable sense of how light in a region progresses.

That she was attractive to him seemed beside the point, since he was too close to his own motives to see them.

When the workers arrive there seems to be an urgency in the air which might be traced to their employer's anxiety over money.

The earth has been striped with zones which attempt to remove the fluid nature of time and the spherical motion of space.

Looking aside, askance, looking indirectly, trying not to look, concentrating forward but remaining aware of the periphery are means of seeing the potential of dimensions beyond the usual four (five).

The darkness of the street may have been influenced by how far away from home it was.

Any set of regulations creates some disharmony.

When he awoke all of the appliances were gone.

Cubans living in the U.S. are not often the same as Cubans living in Cuba.

The boiling of water was a way of measuring the progression of light and shadow through the western windows.

Going just past the point.

Yet at night the ticking could not be heard, despite the intense quiet of the area.

TEN

The most impolite thing would be to break down crying.

Any pressure can't be seen as automatically bad.

Workers removed the refrigerator; workers will bring it back.

The thought that any single act might ease his anxiety.

The reward for an otherwise terrible night had been a sex dream of incredible sensation with a porno star who resembled all the women he had ever slept with.

Curiously, by the side of the road was a shrine called "Vale of Tears."

They who assembled could not avoid certain competitive gestures although the "fellow feeling" was deemed high by all.

There must have been a road nearby.

Focusing on a sound which is both inside and outside.

They had waited for the others to leave but could barely contain the lust which had been building for weeks.

Someone with Turettes's Syndrome represented a tremendous threat to everyone's privacy; that is until they "understood."

Several of them received calls, many received important-looking pieces of mail.

They had been careless by leaving debris all over the "worksite" which, after they left, became again a "bedroom."

A rhythm, an equalizer.

For reasons he couldn't explain, watching his own ejaculation was a great arousal, compounded by her watching.

In many cases choking victims are found in the restroom where they fled to avoid disrupting the banquet.

The general interest in sports was condemned as an indulgence which was too overt.

Rules and entrances, hours and duties, having tasks generated from the outside.

Or any act of repetition.

He heard her call him; she felt a subtle electric charge; she heard him call her; he felt a secret peristalsis.

ELEVEN

Having a tune and distracted.

There is no limit, yet as dark as they knew it to be.

If each living electron, or a vibrating country road.

Given what they wished was so, an attachment to certain central ideas and generosity of spirit were ascribed to several of the attendants.

When geometry strikes, no matter how melodic.

No text but subtext.

Hurtling through space for example.

Comfort itself, in both the evocable and nonevocable states.

The way light on metal, ink in grooves.

The way details then generalities.

The way music, sometimes beside the point.

The way a crumb savored at the end of the day.

The way brevity.

The way gravity.

Opening his farmhouse they were surprised to find her collection of rare art prints purchased for us by your anonymous group.

Every contingency can be planned for, they claimed, but not every one.

Even if the text is completely or partially misunderstood.

When, without warning, the unidentified bird raised its call an octave.

Time, they complained, confused them: palpability.

Each step without the light brought his eyes into sharper focus so that soon his memory had returned and he could see the elections clearly, as if they had happened yesterday.

TWELVE

Waiting in sunlight after a week of rain.

Though only a coincidence, their leaving together in the evening and returning together in the morning.

When the boat left a heavy fog made the journey seem impossible.

Forest, meadow / shoreline, ocean.

Her face was so familiar a fiction was invented.

Sometimes kelp, floating on the surface, heaves with the swells in a kind of respiration.

Red began to show through the density of greens.

Only once had she switched the name tags, but couldn't recall whether it was to be near or away from him.

Sometimes sleeping is aided by the rocking and swaying.

Formulas can also have a liberating effect.

A family of foxes, Yellow Shafted Flickers, deer, large black ants, crows, woodchucks, blue jays, squirrels, possums, wasps, a pony, the rumor of a black bear, robins, several kinds of spiders, a porcupine, newts, frogs, chipmunks, crickets.

Her references to actual experiences with ghosts may or may not have been an invitation to come in.

Being able to see the coastal islands from shore was one way of testing the hypothesis.

The nights could be so dark that any sound would take on extraordinary volume or unbearable significance.

Knowing it would be temporary.

Sea lions, gulls, garibaldi, cormorants, grey whales, marlin, nudibranchs, spiny lobsters, the fear of great white sharks, spinner dolphins, eagle rays, moray eels, horn sharks, kelp bass, a flounder, smelt, pelicans.

Even when the inevitable clouds caused moments of coolness, the rocks remained warm into the night.

Perhaps it had been her voice, his clumsiness, her distance, his eyes, her posture, his voice, her clumsiness, his distance, her eyes, his posture.

Forests, of kelp forests of birches.

In examining the way items in a list create a separate context.

THIRTEEN

To awaken at 3 a.m. with an important mission.

His parents saw him on the elevator.

Supposing any of the people in the party had known the general activity outside their departments.

It's not the temperature, he told them, it's the time.

The system of elevators was not linear, and the resultant complications made it impossible to return to a place just left.

Someone from his childhood who had died long ago was waiting with a woman named Principle.

By then it was day.

Entering the party he noticed that, as usual, he was naked.

It was a digital system, random access, but in the elevator the right number was impossible to find.

As happens with the dead, the friend was the same age now as he had been when they had last seen each other.

What the mission was remained abstract, but of course he couldn't see that.

Principle posed as a waitress in order to steal food, pizza as it turned out.

Somehow the idea that this was all happening on a large and mobile stage did not occur to anyone.

Although his parents knew the lesbian hosts of the party.

Obviously, in daylight, poverty was a key concern, something the dead would be immune to.

The intrusions of allegory would have seemed uncalled for.

He thought of the late hour as similar to being underwater, but why any particular simile.

Despite the cleverness of their plan, they never felt free of suspicion.

On all of the floors was great activity of many, unrelated types.

He alone seemed to move among the contexts.

FOURTEEN

Pile all the dishes up and make each person take one.

Gather at the foot of the landing strip and take off all clothing; wait for a plane to take off; wait for a plane to land; dig a square hole as deep as it is wide; bury the clothes.

Circle 12 times around the meadow, nine times around the house, circle six times from the entrance to the gate post, three times from the kitchen to the room, circle the circumference of the room 30 times, circle the center of the room 1,944 times.

Carry water up the steepest hill; place a living leaf on each of 30 flat stones arranged in a trapezoid; wait for the leaves to dry; while waiting eat only what comes into the circle created by observers who have come along; place one drop of water on each of the leaves.

Put pepper on a page, fold the page, open a shirt worn by someone of the opposite sex.

Find loam by digging for it; take a shovelful and spread it over the floor of the bedroom.

Each day for a year place an ounce of black bread on a field in the same spot; take gravel or sand from that spot each day; store the gravel or sand on the second shelf of a five-shelved bureau; each day return the gravel or sand gathered two days earlier to the spot from which it was taken.

Put the fork at the top side of the plate, the knife at the right side of the plate, the spoon at the bottom side of the plate, the napkin on the left side of the plate and exchange the fork with the knife, the knife with the spoon, the napkin with the fork, the fork with the napkin, the spoon with the knife, the napkin with the spoon, the fork with the knife; sprinkle crushed trilobite fossils over the plate, fork, knife, spoon and napkin.

Paint each fifth tree with a five inch equilateral triangle of the same color as the tree it is covering.

Sit in a chair in the corner of a room and pronounce silently the same word for fifteen minutes.

Open the blanket on the pile of earth; place a handful of earth in the center of the blanket; fold the blanket into a diamond shape; unfold the blanket; remove the earth and replace it with new earth; fold the blanket into a triangle; unfold the blanket; remove the earth and replace it with new earth; fold the blanket into a square; open the blanket and place a small log in the center; roll the blanket and log and earth into a tight cylinder.

Each day sit in front of a white piece of paper and, using a pen which will always have the same color ink, write upon the paper until it is covered with characters.

At the western-most extension of land collect a shell with at least one sharp edge; travel to a pine forest at the tree line; define a rectangle 25 meters wide and 50 meters long; with the shell scrape gently at the bark of each tree within the rectangle; save whatever material has been scraped from the trees using an eelskin pouch.

Learn and memorize the word for wink in every language and every dialect of every language spoken on earth; never speak any of the words.

Stare into the mirror at 11 a.m. and repeat your name 3,000 times.

Collect window putty from every glazier in Los Angeles, New York, London, Rome and Paris; place a speck of each sample onto a salted, 2 x 2 card; place all the cards on the fifth shelf of a Louis XIV armoire, locking the outer door with a nickel plated key.

At the end of every day for three decades, list each thing accomplished, no matter how small, during that day.

Invent a color code for the English Language; using the code, paint the Chapman translations of the Iliad and the Odyssey on the undersides of all the freeway overpasses in California; start over with the Iliad if necessary.

Place one inch squares of scotch tape over all horizontal surfaces while maintaining an air of preoccupation.

Erase the word "the" from each departmental sign in the closest city with a population over one million; take a before and after photograph of each sign; shred each photo and soak the shreddings in a mixture of Pacific Ocean water, water from the Arno river, flour and epoxy cement; clear an acre of desert and dig, in the exact center, a twenty foot, capital, Gil Sans A; fill the A with the soaked shreds of the photos.

FIFTEEN

Angular momentum, their field expressed, a late night, low light.

Than food thefts remarkably planned.

Even levitation, opened as a lover, this process lightening, quiet.

Periodic lapses, the joy of the opaque.

But not of the idea. A calm departure. This will be remembered by you as the exception. Toning it down they called it. Where interference or you tell us how it feels. These moments spent such quiet, but such stillness, just looking.

The voices that received them are imagined.

Even marking the particulars because these would be the ways back in, tonal or visual, taxonomies, steps.

The pieces move around without order but each is considered and placed elsewhere.

So near the window only streaks so quickly only fragments.

It was the problem of topicality not in the sounds allowed to filter in but somehow in what was missing, world without end, an entity overlooked.

The way only images of people had been left.

You time the corner and the whole landscape disappears: so even if you wanted to return.

Any means to silence thought.

Determined as to levels of attention reads: meaning, but the idea of not being special, the humanness of that.

The skin had been turned tight: pores showed that were never known before. Once the truck left it was safe again to look.

Just hearing them say the same words, a lamprey exhumed from the abyssal plain sputtering ink from the too pressed pen.

Printing in the low registers, there had been no maze, no assistance, what was called solitude was just that and here, as we should have known, a temporary blind; we had been seen.

Trapped. A bellows. Internal rhyme. Though rumors. Forest edge reverberating. I had this idea then it was autumn again. Bellows. Following that point. Facility. Distant reports. The tree line, too dark sky. Edge echoes.

Thought the form itself.

Thought the form alone.

SIXTEEN

At a certain temperature moisture in the air will condense into fog.

Remembering a certain quote is not the same as finding it.

The influence of certain "lifestyles" seems to demand being repeated in the art that emerges from them.

It's not the question, it's not the agenda.

As the group altered the atmosphere shifted from easy camaraderie to slightly forced conviviality.

No amount of music would dampen their expectation, and yet time would pass.

She listened to his heart for an entire night before declaring her findings.

Unfortunately, the details of the conversations could never be recalled; fortunately, there were several people present capable of inventing new parts for everyone.

Somehow water always works its way in somehow.

Neither in dense fog nor in bright moonlight was the forest disturbing.

Dialogue on aesthetic issues is sometimes uncomfortably disruptive.

And yet expectation can lead to misapprehensions.

It is always easier to develop tolerances for things which are offensive if the offenses are committed by the wealthy.

Some of these lines may need to be rearranged by either the writer or the reader.

It was only the need to keep the interior distinct from the exterior that caused them to clean.

While ordinarily the "classics" played little or no role.

Among the pleasures of the flesh should be added bird watching.

Certain times of day in certain weather with certain people of certain beliefs.

Although the list as a mode of expression has not been overlooked, it has not been exhausted as a valuable tool.

Only at certain times does description become a negative part of the experience.

SEVENTEEN

It is not a matter of working out a problem so much as it is simply letting external causes change the context of the problem.

Sometimes the ideal circumstances are not possible.

At first he felt slighted but later felt honored.

The time immediately leading up to an anticipated occasion and the time at which the occasion's end is visible.

Wanting to continue and being able to continue.

During the month shadows remained constant but factors which did or did not diffuse them were variable.

Arrogance, youth and mediocrity form one such intolerable combination.

The benefits of having a screen outweigh the disadvantages of looking through it.

Although the particular circumstances of the dream remained unavailable, the locations and atmosphere were so clear it was as if they "had really happened."

Remembering with pleasure the way a group of strangers.

Giving someone a stolen idea.

And how with others the attraction is immediate.

Gradually the exercises meant to relax or acclimatize were no longer thought of.

Friends in another city were unaware of how expensive their requests were.

Maneuvers which appear balletic and graceful.

Density as a method and those who are intolerant of the dense.

The sensation of her chest on his chest was not the same to her as the sensation of his chest on her's was to him.

Those things which can only be explained by contradiction.

In fact evolution, even of something small.

No one else could tell, the series had not been set, her overture had been understood, the people spoke easily with each other, no one else could tell, his own voice, the series, her envoy.

EIGHTEEN

Sediments floating upwards.

Every character had been coded, each plot element lettered.

Returning home they noticed a light on in a room they never entered.

The power of a title should never be underestimated.

In this case the police would be of no help.

He had come to a dense forest and suddenly remembered all the stories which gave dimensions to his fears.

Robbing good ideas of their power.

Sunlight actually did "dazzle" their eyes.

A large staff of researchers were assembled to find support for her radical ideas.

It is not the historicity of the Iliad.

Catalysts are by their nature things which command respect, fear even.

At first they thought the planets were rapidly moving retrograde, then the airplane landed.

Fear of ghosts isn't exactly fear.

Naming being an important accomplishment of this civilization.

The crow walked away down the trail until it was just a sheen of black and silver.

Balance only seemed to be an issue.

The slow, contemplative pace, the long pauses during which thoughts of all kinds.

Naming but also the method of naming.

They searched for a clue.

Their ages had nothing to do with it.

NINETEEN

Another in a series of rainstorms.

The town's river also effected.

Change and changeability being highly valued qualities.

Knowing the problem, for example "human warmth."

Using certain terms only clouds the issue.

They had come to understand that expectation.

Halfway through the car trip she slammed on the brakes remembering a book she had left at home.

None of them had been embarrassed to express a frank opinion although forthrightness did not prevent animosities.

"I've accepted obscurity; it's part of my strategy," she told him.

Now that structure can be found in anything.

He was sorry that his commitment to a certain idea was so strong that he had not dedicated his books to anyone.

The earth and sun maintain relative positions, the trees are stable in their fixed locations on a predictably rotating planet, but wind moving clouds and pressures causing winds and clouds, and heat from the sun and seasonal variations of angles of incidence.

Some said it was pollution, others that it was algae.

They didn't exactly avoid each other.

Yet even obscurity.

But they are all really for you, he told her.

From mode to mode and from element to element within each mode, only a vague tone and a freely defined structure were consistent.

She debated whether to return or attempt to buy another copy when she arrived at her destination.

Who would be waiting and who would be gone.

The choice seemed to be between courtesy and confrontation.

TWENTY

The time was so short.

On the first sunny afternoon in a month they dedicated then launched the new boat.

The way a palm shows its immediate history, or any tree in fact.

Voices could be heard from their hiding places.

Several stops needed to be made in preparation for this, the biggest festival of the year.

Back in their country where the average expectancy was so much less.

The sound of passing airplanes in the middle of a quiet day gave him a feeling of comfort that he could never understand.

Understanding that, among other things, hope and anticipation.

Whether through selfishness or guilt the neighbors had taken tremendous risks to save his life.

Several of the youth service organizations were sending representatives as a kind of gesture.

Even so, the field which had been brown and fallow.

Of course, no one could promise good weather, but at least now, as they packed their bags, everything seemed to bode well.

She was saddened to find the field mouse, which she had been feeding, dead on the area rug.

At night, dressed in black, they felt able to recede into the shadows and remain undetected.

Given enough food and sufficient party favors.

It was true that in other regions seasons were marked through other signs.

The way that keeping a journal could be seen as preserving space and time.

Wasps, which seemed to awaken with the heat, became lethargic in no relation to the humans near them.

Yet it was impossible for either of them to feel truly invisible.

They had been certain that Mr. Q had promised them the ball, so certain that they purchased new clothes and wrote letters to their relatives in cities far away.